Is Wise Owl Wise?

Written and illustrated by Shoo Rayner

Rigby®

A Harcourt Achieve Imprint

www.Rigby.com

1-800-531-5015

This is a story about an owl, who *looked* very wise and *looked* very clever.

This owl hunted for his food at night.

In the day, he slept on the best branch of his tree.

But when he slept, Owl did not shut his eyes. He kept them open just a little bit, and that made him look very clever.

The animals in the forest saw him
and said, "He looks so wise and
looks so clever."

There was a pond in the forest, and in the pond lived many frogs. One summer it didn't rain, and all the water in the pond dried up.

The frogs got very hot. "What shall we do?" they asked. "Let us go and ask Owl. He'll tell us what to do. He looks so wise and looks so clever."

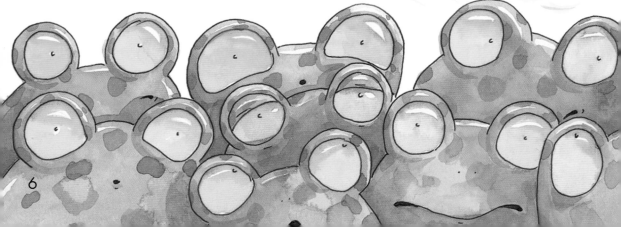

The frogs told Owl about the pond.
"What shall we do?" asked
the frogs.
"What do you think you should
do?" hooted Owl.

"We think that we should hide under big, cold stones and wait for the rain," said the frogs.

"Then do it, do it, do," said Owl.

So the frogs hid under big, cold stones and waited for the rain. When the rain came, the pond filled with water, and the frogs were happy again.

In the fall, some of the birds were cold and hungry.

"What shall we do?" they asked.

"Let us go and ask Owl," the other birds answered. "He'll tell us what to do. He looks so wise and looks so clever." So they went and asked Owl.

"What do you think you should do?" hooted Owl.

"We think we should fly away, to where the sun shines every day," said the birds. "Then do it, do it, do," said Owl.

So they flew away, to where the sun shines every day, and the birds were happy again.

When winter came to the forest, it began to snow, covering some of the animals. They were very cold. "What shall we do?" they asked.

"Let us go and ask Owl. He'll tell us what to do. He looks so wise and looks so clever."

So they went and asked Owl.

"What do you think you should do?" hooted Owl.

"We think that we should sleep until spring," said the squirrels and the badgers.

"We think that we should put on warm winter coats," said the foxes and the rabbits.

"We think that we should keep each other warm," said the little birds.

"We think that we should keep a hole open in the ice," said the ducks.

"Then do it, do it, do," said Owl.

So, the squirrels and the badgers slept until spring. The foxes and the rabbits grew warm winter coats. The little birds found a hole in a tree and kept each other warm. The ducks took turns sitting in a hole in the ice so they could get to their food. The animals were all happy.

"Owl is so wise and so clever," they said. "He told us what to do, and he was right!"

But Owl hadn't really told them anything. For Owl was not really wise nor really clever. Owl was asleep on the best branch of his tree and dreaming that he was catching mice.